P R E S E N T E D   T O :

_____

F R O M :

_____

D A T E :

_____

OUR TRIP ACROSS AMERICA · BRUCE & STAN

Stories We Heard About Hope

ON OUR TRIP ACROSS AMERICA

Bruce Bickel &
Stan Jantz

Contents

Behind Every Life
is a Story.

Introduction

We're two ordinary guys, but we had an extraordinary adventure. We spent the summer driving across the country. Now, that event isn't extraordinary in itself. In fact, many people have performed the feat. But most folks drive across country in an attempt to complete the task as quickly as possible. The memories of those trips are long hours on the inter-state, fast food wrappers scattered on the car floor, and no personal contact with anyone except the cashiers at the old-fashioned gas stations (the ones that have pumps and don't accept credit cards) and the occasional tollbooth operator. (People who are in a real hurry, or particularly antisocial, save time and avoid contact with even the tollbooth operator by keeping lots of coins in the car and using the "exact change" lane.)

Our trip was different. It extended over three and one-half months, so speed was obviously not an issue. We drove over 10,000 miles (which proves we didn't take the short route). But the *duration* and *distance* are not what made our trip extraordinary. The most intriguing aspect of our trip was the *people* we met and the *stories* they shared with us about their lives.

The purpose of our trip was to interview people. We were doing the research for a book (*Bruce & Stan Search for the Meaning of Life*), so we spoke with everyone, everywhere (even tollbooth operators and gas station cashiers). We had meaningful conversations with over 1,000 people. (That figure *doesn't* include the people we passed on the street or sat next to on the subway or stood next to in the elevator, with whom we exchanged limited pleasantries. Actually, we didn't even exchange pleasantries with the people in the elevators. We didn't want to break the unwritten rule of elevator etiquette, which prohibits talking or making eye contact.)

We expected to learn a lot about the meaning of life by talking to people (and we did). We learned so much, it could fill a book (and it has). But the unexpected pleasure was hearing the personal stories of the people we met. We heard fascinating stories about people. Some of the stories involved tragic events; some were encouraging. All of them were life changing—for the people who actually lived the stories and for us as we heard them.

Our lives will not be the same because of the people we met and the stories we heard. If for no other reason, we have a greater appreciation for people because we learned this very important lesson: *Behind every life is a story!*

What makes these stories so amazing is that they involve regular people. We didn't talk to any celebrities. Just plain folk. People like us . . . and you. (This assumes that you aren't chauffeured around in a limo and that you don't live in a mansion. If you're like us, you're more concerned about paying the mortgage than avoiding the paparazzi. In fact, we are only interested in "paparazzi" if it's a new flavor of Ben & Jerry's ice cream.)

In this book we've included several of our favorite stories that we heard while we were "on the road." They all have a common theme of hope. We learned a lot about hope from the people in these stories. Hope is much more than a wish. A wish—whether it's made when you blow out the birthday candles or when you mail in your Publishers' Clearinghouse Sweepstakes form—is nothing more than an expressed desire. A wish doesn't change the way you see your future. But hope does. Instead of looking ahead in life and seeing a hopeless end, the people in these stories looked ahead in life and saw an endless hope. It was their hope that allowed them to see the invisible, feel the intangible, and believe the implausible to achieve the impossible.

We suspect that you'll be inspired by these stories. We were. Maybe they'll motivate you to reflect on your personal stories and the lessons that you can learn from your own life. Maybe they'll make you more interested in the life stories of your friends and your neighbors. Maybe they'll encourage you to be more interested in the people you don't know as well. Remember: *Behind every life is a story!*

Bruce & Stan

The Vision of Hope

We consider ourselves fortunate to have driven through some of the most scenic spots in America. Each region of the country has its own unique splendor, so we don't want to declare any particular area the most beautiful. While we won't declare a winner, we can tell you that one of the finalists for the "Bruce & Stan's Most Spectacular Scenic Wonders" list has got to be Santa Barbara, California. This Spanish-styled town, located about ninety miles north of Los Angeles, is nestled between foothills and some of the most pristine, white sand beaches along the Pacific shoreline. The weather hovers around 70-80 degrees year-round. The air is clear. We're sure the angels are anxious to leave heaven to vacation there.

A few miles up from the beach is the exclusive foothill residential area of Montecito. This is a community of large estates, some belonging to long-time residents, others acquired by recent arrivals from places like Hollywood or Silicon Valley. In the midst of these multi-million dollar mansions sits the 133-acre campus of Westmont College. Westmont is a residential liberal arts college where a small but diverse student body has assembled from across the country. While attaining a national reputation for its academic rigor and excellence (the U.S. News & World Report

Westmont students enjoy class outdoors.

survey ranks it as one of the leading national liberal arts colleges in America), Westmont is distinctively Christian.

With the respect that Westmont enjoys in both academic and religious circles, and considering its scenic surroundings, it came as no surprise to us that Westmont College manages to attract leading scholars to its faculty and top-level administrators to its staff. But apparently, those factors haven't been the main attraction over the past two decades. To the extent that Westmont's rise in prominence can be attributed to any single factor, it would have to be the College's president, Dr. David K. Winter.

Dr. Winter's accomplishments have brought national recognition to himself as well as to Westmont College.

• He has brought his humble and effective leadership skills to many of the prestigious organizations within American higher education. He has served as the President of the Independent Colleges of Southern California, Chair of the Association of Independent California Colleges and Universities, Chair of the Christian College Consortium, and Director of the National Association of Independent Colleges and Universities. He served as chair of the Senior Commission of the Western Association of Schools and Colleges and as a Director for the Council on Higher Education Accreditation based in Washington, D.C.

- He shows the students of Westmont that following Christ involves service to others. He is active in his church, and he works tirelessly in the community, having volunteered with the Salvation Army, the United Way, and Rotary. The Santa Barbara Council on Alcoholism and Drug Abuse named him as one of their 1998 "Twelve Men of Distinction." *The Santa Barbara News-Press* has honored him with its Lifetime Achievement Award and he received the Distinguished Community Service Award for 2000 from the Santa Barbara Chapter of the Anti-Defamation League.

For many years, David Winter
has followed 2 Corinthians 12:9
as his guiding verse:

But he said to me,
"My grace is sufficient for
you, for my power is made
perfect in weakness."
Therefore I will boast all the
more gladly about my
weaknesses, so that Christ's
power may rest on me.

Perhaps more than his competencies and his service, Dr. Winter has been recognized for the quality of his character. It is his magnetic personality and gracious nature that have drawn an outstanding faculty and staff to Westmont College. His integrity and humility have set a tone on campus that has been emulated by the students. But the strength of his character is evident to more than just those on the Westmont campus. A 1986 survey of higher education officials and scholars conducted by Bowling Green State University and funded by the Exxon Foundation listed Dr. Winter as one of the 100 most effective college leaders in the United States. In 1999, the John Templeton Foundation selected Dr. Winter as one of fifty college presidents who have exercised leadership in character development. With class, dignity, and a sense of humor, he displays a Christ-like character that is evident to all who know him.

Dr. Winter has served as the president of Westmont College for twenty-four years. After all that time, he knows the paths of the campus well enough to walk them with his eyes closed. That's pretty much what he has been doing for the last few years after he suddenly lost his eyesight.

David Winter and his wife, Helene.

It was the week following commencement in the Spring of 1998. David and his wife, Helene, were preparing to take a vacation when he noticed a few grey dots in his field of vision. Within a few days, those dots grew into larger blind spots. After a few weeks, he had lost 80–90 percent of his sight. At the peak of his presidency, at the beginning

We noticed that people
are very careful with their use of certain
terminology at Westmont College.
They make a distinction between words
like sight, seeing, vision, and outlook.
To us, those words seemed fairly
interchangeable. But at Westmont,
their meaning is quite different because:
David Winter sees primarily darkness,
but his outlook is bright.
While his sight is obscured, he
has tremendous vision.

of launching Westmont into a $47 million fund-raising campaign, and at the verge of accomplishing some long-term goals for the College, Dr. Winter became blind.

The doctors call it non-arthritic ischemic optic neuropathy. That's the technical term. Here's the translation: David Winter sees grainy darkness. In sufficient light, he can identify shapes and he can slightly read enlarged print. But he has come to grips with the fact that he is essentially blind and that his sight will never be restored.

People handle tragedy in their lives in different ways. Some crumble under the crushing devastation. Others withdraw to deal with their circumstances in a private manner. David Winter handles his personal trauma in the same way that he has lived his life for the preceding two decades: openly, honestly, and in front of 1,200 students. You see, David Winter knew that it is relatively easy to model the Christian life when all of your circumstances appear to be fortunate ones. With the loss of his sight, David Winter knew he had the opportunity to demonstrate how to follow Christ when the circumstances of life become brutal.

Dr. Winter is now in this third academic year without sight. Some believe he is more effective than ever as a college president, but David says he has become a better person. He says his disability has made him more sensitive to the needs of others. He finds himself much more appreciative of the beauty in the world and of the kindness that people have extended to him, his wife, and the College. He says he is

Dr. Winter chats with Westmont students.

closer to God, and for that reason he is thankful for the loss of his eyesight.

In a quiet moment with her husband, Helene once reminded David that she was praying for a miracle — a miracle that his sight would be restored. David whispered back: "A miracle has already happened. I have the miracle of God's peace and hope in my heart about all of this."

The way in which David and Helene handle his disability has made it much easier for those on campus to deal with it. The Winters approach this change in circumstances with the same graciousness and self-effacing humor that they have always displayed.

● Although he could manage in most situations without a white cane, Dr. Winter uses one. At first he struggled with admitting to himself that he had a disability. Now he carries his white cane with no embarrassment that he has a physical limitation. And he is quick to add, "Also, I am particularly interested in making sure that people driving by know that I can't see."

- Both David and Helene confess that mealtime is an adventure. David tells the story of scooping a forkful of food from his plate into his mouth, only to discover he was eating a pad of butter.

- We were walking with Dr. Winter as he exited a building and walked out into the sunshine on the beautiful Westmont campus. He removed his glasses and cleaned them with his handkerchief. Then he turned to us and said, "I don't know why I do that. It doesn't make any difference."

- We sat in on a committee meeting where Dr. Winter was the moderator. There was a fairly strong division of opinion by the members on a particular issue. Dr. Winter asked those in favor to raise their hands. Then he asked those opposed to raise their hands. Then Helene jumped to her feet and said, "Why are you asking. You can't see the responses." The laughter that ensued diffused the tension, and the committee arrived at a decision made with the consensus of all members.

We don't know if Dr. Winter has become a more effective leader than he was before his sight loss, but he certainly hasn't been slowed down or distracted by self-pity.

God uses hardships to teach us lessons. David and Helene Winter would certainly testify to that. As they continue to learn more about God each day through this experience, Dr. Winter takes every opportunity to convey what he has learned to the students at Westmont. After all, he is the consummate educator, and he doesn't want to miss this teaching opportunity. While he presents to the Westmont students new insights from his circumstances as he learns them, there appears to be one recurring theme in what he teaches them:

God doesn't promise that we'll be free from hard times; but He does promise He will be with us during them. God keeps that promise, and David Winter has the hope to prove it.

———————————

There is one hymn that has become particularly meaningful to David Winter since the loss of his eyesight in the Spring of 1998. As you read the lyrics, we're sure you'll understand why.

Be Thou My Vision

(An ancient Irish hymn, translated by Mary E. Byrne)

Be Thou my vision, O Lord of my heart;
Naught be all else to me, save that Thou art—
Thou my best thought, by day or by night,

28

Waking or sleeping, Thy presence my light.

Be Thou my Wisdom, and Thou my true Word;
I ever with Thee and Thou with me, Lord;
Thou my great Father, I thy true son,
Thou in me dwelling, and I with Thee one.

Riches I heed not, nor man's empty praise,
Thou mine inheritance, now and always;
Thou and Thou only, first in my heart,
High King of heaven, my Treasure Thou art.

High King of heaven, my victory won,
May I reach heaven's joys, O bright heaven's Sun!
Heart of my own heart, whatever befall;
Still be my Vision, O Ruler of all.

Hope to Win

Whenever you leave home for any length of time, as we did in the summer of 2000 to travel across America, you tend to look for things that give you a sense of connection. It's important to connect with home, of course, and we did that on a daily basis using our cell phones and email (isn't this digital age wonderful?). But we also found that establishing some kind of daily connection with the world was necessary.

Communicating with our wives gave us news about the details of family and friends, but never once did they tell us, "The price of hog futures is up today," or "The Yankees won again last night." It was up to us to find out the latest in current events.

There are many ways to gather the news of the day when you're on the road. You can turn on one of those morning shows, but they're pretty much vehicles for people like Katie Couric and Matt Lauer (the stars of NBC's *Today Show*) to showcase their perkiness and good-natured personalities. The daily news roundup is fairly shallow.

You can always buy a local newspaper, but we since we were generally on our way out of town each morning, we didn't need to know about the local happenings. The other option—and this is the one we found most valuable—is to purchase a copy of *USA Today,* also known as the nation's newspaper.

USA Today is a marvel of modern ingenuity and technology. While you're sleeping, reporters from all over the world assemble news and stories and write them all up in a way that holds your attention without bogging you down. They cover everything from politics to business to entertainment to sports, and it's all right there waiting for you each morning, no matter where you are, in all its full-color glory for just fifty cents. Is this a great country, or what?

In addition to connecting you with world and national events, *USA Today* puts you in touch with some very fascinating people and their stories. One of the stories that made the biggest impression on us all summer was the story of Brandon Slay, a young man from Amarillo, Texas who did something few Americans—and nobody from Texas—have ever done: he won an Olympic gold medal in freestyle wrestling.

When we first read about Brandon in *USA Today,* he was profiled as an Olympic hopeful in the 76kg/167.5 pound weight class. Normally we wouldn't look twice at an article about a wrestler, but right in the middle of the story was a great photo of Brandon sitting on the tailgate of his pickup truck. He was wearing the customary cowboy

I strain to reach the end
of the race and receive
the prize through which God,
through Christ Jesus,
is calling us up to heaven.

PHILIPPIANS 3:14

boots and Levis (customary for Texans, that is), but what caught our eye was his T-shirt. Emblazoned on the front were the words, "Jesus Christ is Life" with the reference of John 14:6.

We scanned the nearly full-page article with great interest. Was Brandon the real deal, or was this a guy who paid God lip service only (or in this case, T-shirt service)? It didn't take us long to understand that Brandon was a very special young man indeed. The article related how Brandon was a two-time NCAA runner-up as an Ivy League wrestler (amazingly, Texas has no college wrestling programs), and a graduate of the University of Pennsylvania's Wharton School of Business to boot (no pun intended). The *USA Today* article focused on his attempt to make the U.S. Olympic wrestling team at the Olympic trials in Dallas.

"When I found out two years ago that the Olympic trials

would be in Dallas," Brandon said, "I just had this peace of mind come over me that it was my destiny to make the Olympic team in my home state." Little did Brandon know how prophetic his words would be. Not only did he become the champion of the Olympic trials in his weight class, but a little more than three months later he became the champion of the world. And he did it in a way that clearly involved both destiny and hope.

There was destiny in Brandon's Olympic odyssey because no one could have written a more dramatic script for his road to glory. As for the hope, there's no way Brandon could have kept his dream alive without it. Competing at the national level in freestyle wrestling is one thing, especially when you battle other amateurs. (Keep in mind that this is NOT the WWF. This is real wrestling between guys who do other things for a living.) When you get to the international level, you're thrown into the ring with seasoned athletes who are generally sponsored by their home countries so they can concentrate full-time on their sport.

PHOTO: TIM TUSHLA, W.I.N. MAGAZINE

In one of the early rounds of the Olympic games, Brandon defeated Bouvaissa Saitiev of Russia, a world wrestling legend and the defending Olympic champion. Then Brandon beat Gennadiy Laliyev of Kazakhstan to advance to the semi-finals. Remarkably, the soft-spoken Texan won his semi-final match and found himself in the gold medal round against German freestyle wrestler Alexander Leipold, who was competing in his fourth Olympic games.

Brandon Slay finishes a takedown on Bouvaissa Saitiev of Russia.

That's when Brandon's destiny seemed to come to an end, and with it his hope for Olympic gold. Leipold defeated him in a close match.

Brandon accepted his second-place finish with class, while the German did back flips and handsprings in celebration. The unlikely dream was over. Or so everybody thought, including Brandon. Then, less than a month after the Sydney Olympics were a fading memory, something even more unlikely happened. The International Olympic Committee announced that Leipold had been stripped of his gold medal due

Brandon with Alex O'Brien at the opening ceremonies in Sydney.

> Great works are performed not by strength but by perseverance.
>
> WILLIAM WILBERFORCE

to a positive drug test, making Brandon Slay the Olympic champion. His destiny, which had taken a detour, was back on track. His hope was fulfilled.

"At first, it was a relief, then I had peace of mind knowing my ultimate athletic dream had been accomplished," Brandon said at an official Olympic awards ceremony staged in New York City (hosted by the good-natured Matt Lauer). "This medal is not tainted at all," he told Lauer in an interview. "I think it has opened up a wonderful forum for children to learn that if you break the law and you take drugs, that not only can you lose your life, but you can lose your lifelong dream."

Brandon concluded the interview by giving credit to the source of his hope and the motivation for his dream. "It feels wonderful," he said. "I want to thank God for all the blessings He has given me. I'd like to dedicate this gold medal to [Coach] Dave Schultz, who sparked my Olympic dream."

Brandon enjoys some post-Olympic recreation.

No doubt Brandon's own story of hope will spark the dreams of others. It certainly inspired us!

Some people dream
of worthy accomplishments.
Other people wake
up and work hard to achieve them.
The difference is initiative.

OUR TRIP ACROSS AMERICA · BRUCE & STAN

Hope for the Hopeless

Each year millions of people visit Washington, D. C., and our guess is that every one of them is inspired by the stunning beauty and the absolute power of the place.

There's a reason why Washington is so beautiful: it was planned that way. Most cities develop rather haphazardly as their population grows. There's usually no rhyme or reason for the way streets and buildings are laid out. Not so with Washington. In 1791 a French architect by the name of Pierre Charles L'Enfant designed the city block by block. He laid out the building sites so the prime branches of government would be featured and named the major streets after the states that played the biggest role in the nation's building process, such as Massachusetts, Virginia, and Pennsylvania.

The majestic Capitol Building is situated on a hill overlooking a great grassy mall. At the other end of the mall in a straight line from the Capitol is the Lincoln Memorial. Between these two unmistakable landmarks is the world's most famous obelisk, the Washington Monument. To the north is the White House, the oldest and best known federal building in Washington. To the south is the graceful Jefferson Memorial. When you take it all in like we did on a simple walking tour, you appreciate Washington as a fitting capital for the most powerful nation on earth.

The Jefferson Memorial.

That's the other thing you notice in Washington: the power. You don't have to go to Capitol Hill and walk the halls of Congress like we did to get this sense. The images of influence are everywhere. Besides somber buildings with important names like the Federal Bureau of Investigation, the Department of Justice, the Internal Revenue Service, and the Supreme Court, you see powerful looking people with dark suits and brief cases get in and out of limousines on just about every corner. Dozens of embassies, some housed in former mansions, welcome foreign dignitaries every day of the week. Everyone who comes to Washington knows that this is the place to be if you want to make a difference in the world and in your career. That's power.

We were getting rather light headed from all the beauty and power of Washington (we wondered if we had the early signs of Potomac fever) and were concerned that our image of the District was getting rather slanted. We figured there had to be more to the city than the elected officials, government staff, political advisors, lawyers, and journalists. That's when we decided to pay a visit to Rick and Debbie Yorgey.

Rick and Debbie are just as sharp as anyone we met on Capitol Hill. If they wanted to work with people of influence, they would fit right into the power mix of Washington's elite. But Rick and his wife Debbie have chosen a different path that leads to a very different part of the nation's capital, a part that few visitors ever see.

To get to the Yorgey's row house, you don't drive on one of those dramatic boulevards named for a state. You take Thirteenth Street north to an area known as Brightwood, where the houses touch each other on each side. You would call it a working class neighborhood, except there are an unusual number of adult men standing around doing nothing in particular. Most of them are black.

By contrast (and it is a contrast in this neighborhood), Rick and Debbie are white. They came here nine years ago, not because of the affordable housing, but because they wanted to befriend, help, and give themselves to people far removed from the beauty and the power of Washington. The Yorgeys invited us to join them for dinner, and we asked them to tell us their story.

"Our mandate has always been James 1:27," said Rick. "Pure and lasting religion in the sight of God our Father means that we must care for orphans and widows in their troubles and refuse to let the world corrupt us." Add to that "single mothers," "drug

Caring means

being truly concerned

for others.

ONYOUROWN.COM

addicts,"and "the unemployed," and you begin to get a sense of what the Yorgeys are here in Washington to do. But how could all of this exist just a few miles from the city center, where the nation's most powerful people routinely go about their business?

Rick explained that there are really two Washingtons. There is the public Washington that everyone sees on television and visits on vacation. And then there are the many neighborhoods suffering from poverty and crime. Between these two worlds is a great social and economic disparity. The truth is, most people who work in the halls of power leave the city at the end of the day and drive to one of the many affluent suburbs in Virginia and Maryland, the two states that surround the District of Columbia, in which Washington is completely contained.

The "white flight" started in the 1950s, when Washington became the first major American city with a black majority. By 1990 blacks comprised two-thirds of the city's residents, and disadvantaged areas (such as the one where the Yorgeys live) became subject to a plague of drugs and violence. As the murder rate climbed, Washington—the capital of the most powerful country in the world—became one of America's deadliest cities.

Meanwhile the suburbs, spurred on by the growth of Washington's burgeoning government and energetic high-tech industry, flourished. During our stay, we picked up a copy of the *Washington Post* and read that Fairfax County, Virginia, just across the Potomac River from Washington D. C., has become the nation's richest community. "Fairfax is now the first jurisdiction in the country with a median household income topping $90,000," the article said. "Fairfax County continues to push the boundaries of affluence."

"We don't do anything special," Rick said. "Our calling is to be in the neighborhood, to attend the local schools, worship at our neighborhood church, and reach out the best way we can. It hasn't been easy. People have been suspicious of our motives, but one by one God is using us to bring hope and to make a difference."

Washington may be the nation's capital, but it is no different than any other city in America. There is great affluence in our cities, usually generated by some kind of thriving industry concentrated in the city center. But when night falls and it's time to go home, the affluent commute to their homes in the suburbs and their comfortable lives, leaving vast tracts of housing to crumble and decay. Rick told us about the Christian Community Development Association (CCDA), a Chicago-based nonprofit association that seeks to alleviate "the desperate conditions that face the poor in cities across America"

through the "strong commitment and risky actions on the part of ordinary Christians with heroic faith."

That pretty much describes the Yorgeys. They are living examples of people who affirm the dignity of others, motivate them, and help them take responsibility for their lives.

The philosophy of CCDA and the Yorgeys can be summarized in a Chinese poem found on the CCDA Web site:

Go to the people

Live among them

Learn from them

Love them

Start with what they know

Build on what they have:

But of the best leaders

When their task is done

The people will remark

"We have done it ourselves."

This is the way to give people hope who would otherwise never have any. And you don't have to travel to a third world country. Our cities contain all the hopeless people we could possibly help in a lifetime. "God is inviting us to join Him in His work," Rick said. "God is waiting for us to give hope to the hopeless."

OUR TRIP ACROSS AMERICA

BRUCE & STAN

Hope Breaks Free

If you spend lots of time in the big cities of America as a tourist, you'll end up spending lots of time in the back seats of taxicabs. We know, because we did. And we have some sticky substance on most of our Dockers, jeans, and slacks to prove it.

Most cabs are incubators for viral infections and strains of bacteria for which there are no known cures. Most passengers avoid inhaling these air-born, backseat germs by holding their breath from the time they enter the cab until they exit upon reaching their destination. The breath holding isn't a technique that's employed to intentionally avoid diseases; it's just the natural reaction to the stink in most cabs.

If you think we're critical of taxicab hygiene, you're correct. We aren't germ freaks and we aren't particularly finicky. (The mustard stains on Bruce's shirts are proof of that.) But we do think the business of public conveyance deserves as modicum of sanitation. In other words, we don't think the backseat of a cab should look like the inside of a trash dumpster.

Imagine our surprise when we entered an immaculate cab in New Orleans (a city not known for impeccable cleanliness). The smell of Armor-all was in the air (blending nicely with the evergreen scent from the "I Love Jesus" freshener dangling from the rear-view mirror). The floor had been vacuumed, the vinyl seats had been polished, the windows had been cleaned, and the driver had showered. We wondered if we had stumbled into another dimension—kind of a "Bizarro Cab World" where the taxis are the opposite of real life.

We couldn't resist talking to the driver. We knew there must be something different about him because there was certainly something different about his cab. We thought he might be a clean freak. (No, that couldn't be the case because he was living in New Orleans.) This mystery demanded an explanation.

We complimented our driver on the appearance of his cab. He acknowledged our praise with a response that indicated we weren't the first passengers to comment about its cleanliness. We gave him every opportunity to give us a reasonable explanation (like he saved the life of a guy who owns a car-wash so now he gets a lifetime of free washes), but he said nothing. We think he was playing mental games with us. If he was, then he won, because our curiosity couldn't be quelled.

"Okay, we've got to ask," we blurted out. *"Why* is your cab so clean?"

"It's simple," he said. "This cab is my kingdom of God on earth. This is what God has given to me, and driving people is how I serve Him. So, I want it to be as clean as possible. It reflects my attitude about God."

We had heard the expression that cleanliness was next to Godliness, but we had never expected to have an antiseptic angel as a cab driver.

We told you in the Introduction to this book that behind every life is a story. Our cab driver, Michael Williams, is living proof of that statement. As we continued to interrogate him, we were fascinated by his answers. In fact, we kept changing our destination because we didn't want to get out of the cab until he had finished telling us the story of his life.

Michael was born and raised in New Orleans. He said his family had a history of drug use and dealing, and as a young man he followed the family pattern. As a result, he

Having faith in God is more than a belief in His existence. It is turning control of your life over to Him.

was involved with a tough crowd. His misadventures eventually landed him at the wrong place at the wrong time. A murder was committed, and he was the one falsely accused of the killing.

Michael felt that justice would prevail and he would be found innocent. While he was actually guilty of many crimes, this murder was certainly not one of them. While the circumstantial evidence appeared incriminating, he was confident that a good attorney and a fair trial would reveal the truth. But Michael's confidence was misplaced for two reasons: he didn't get a good attorney or a fair trial.

Michael doesn't have any kind remarks to make about attorneys. (Bruce is one, but we didn't disclose that to Michael.) Michael feels about lawyers the same way we feel about taxicabs: most of them are a disgrace. Michael has good reasons to feel that way. He went through three lawyers, and they all failed him. As Michael explained it,

"The first lawyer used up all of my drug money, and didn't do anything. The second lawyer used up all of my mother's money, and didn't do anything. The third lawyer took all of the money that I could borrow from family and friends, and he did even less."

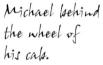

Michael behind the wheel of his cab.

Convicted of first-degree murder, Michael was sent to prison. It was there that he got serious about God and serious about getting out. He studied the Bible and law books with equal vigor. He became a sort of prison paralegal. As the result of his legal research and the pleading he filed, he obtained the reversal of convictions and the release of several other

Get to know God better.
If you make this a priority...
everything else you do
will fall into place.

ONYOUROWN.COM

inmates who had been falsely convicted. And, after eighteen years in prison, he had his own conviction reversed.

Right now you're probably asking yourself the same question we posed to him: "Weren't you bitter when you got out?" "Well, God kept me from being bitter," he said. "In prison I realized all the terrible things I had done without being caught. I was in prison for a crime that I didn't commit, but I deserved to be in prison for what I had actually done."

Freed from prison, Michael went to work in an oil

refinery. He did a little paralegal work on the side and was always looking for odd jobs. A friend who drove a taxi encouraged Michael to drive cabs for a living. God confirmed to Michael that driving a cab was his ministry.

The locals in New Orleans know about Michael. They know his cab is different, but they also know he is a different kind of driver. Michael picks up passengers that other drivers will ignore. Because he considers his driving to be a divine mission, Michael gives rides to the rough and undesirable elements of the New Orleans population. And Michael goes to parts of the city that other drivers ignore. Sometimes this willingness has put his life in danger. On more than one occasion, he suspected that he was being set up to be robbed. But as he often does, Michael talked on these occasions with his passengers about God's love. Each time, the suspected attacker has asked to be dropped off at a spot several blocks before the designated destination where accomplices were waiting to hijack the cab.

Since the time we met him, Michael has started to do his own traveling. At the invitation of a prison ministry, he goes to Texas once a month to tell his story to inmates there.

If you have the chance to visit New Orleans, try to hail Michael's taxi. It won't be difficult to identify him. His cab is the only clean one in town, and he'll be the driver with a shining face of hope.

When people think of New Orleans they automatically think of Bourbon Street.

Street scene in New Orleans.

We had met lots of fascinating people and heard lots of interesting stories by the time we reached the end of our cross-country trip. The settings of almost all these stories were in places we had visited, so we could easily picture the scenery and surroundings in our mind. If we heard a story, we had seen the locale. From the Florida everglades, to the Rocky Mountains, to the amber waves of grain, we had seen it all. All 10,000 miles of it.

Just as we were beginning to impress ourselves with our personal travel experience and expertise (we are easily impressed), we linked up with Jim and Sue De Vries. We tried to amaze them by saying we had driven almost 10,000 miles during the summer. They graciously tried to fake an astonished expression. We came to realize that 10,000 miles doesn't sound too impressive to Jim and Sue. That's because they live in Africa and they return to America as often as possible to visit their three daughters.

Jim and Sue have been missionaries for about thirty years. In addition to Africa, they have lived in Central America and the Philippines. You don't want to brag about your trip to Spartanburg, South Carolina to this couple. They'll enjoy listening to your travelogue because they're so friendly, but you aren't going to be able to top their stories. In case you ever meet them, learn from our mistakes. Our narration about seeing the world's largest ball of earwax in Bozeman, Montana just didn't match the panache of Jim's story about climbing Mt. Kenya.

Realizing that we couldn't compete against Jim and Sue with our own measly travel experiences, we decided to impress them with some of the fascinating stories we had heard along the way. We figured that they had been isolated so long in Kenya that they'd be starving for a good story. So, we laid some of our best stuff on them. We hit them with a few tender stories of love; we blasted them with a couple touching stories of joy; and we pounded them with a story or two about courage. We even pulled out all stops with a few of the stories about hope included in this book.

Jim and Sue listened with great interest as we regaled them with the stories we had collected on our trip. The people sitting around the table with us were also duly impressed. We were just beginning to impress ourselves with our abilities as master storytellers, when Jim uttered those fateful words: "While you were talking, I was reminded of a story I heard." We felt a breeze around the table as everyone quickly turned their heads toward him. We did our best to create a diversion. Bruce made a comment about feeling an earthquake while Stan shook the table with his legs. But we were in California where earthquakes are as commonplace and boring as two guys driving across country. To our chagrin, Jim had captivated everyone's attention as he told a story that had its beginning about fifty years ago in the arid savannah of Northwest Kenya. Jim spoke in such a colorful and descriptive manner we could almost hear the tribal African drums beating in the distance. We can't tell the story as well as Jim did, but it's worth repeating, even if you have to read it in plain, old, boring Bruce and Stan style:

About fifty years ago, an American missionary, Tom Collins, devoted his life to bringing the Bible message to the nomadic tribes of Africa. It was a hard existence. He was required to traverse the dry and desolate Kenyan desert by jeep, and sometimes by foot, to locate their settlements. He was separated from his family for long periods of time. Worst of all, his efforts were met with resistance, and he retired with little to show for his efforts. He

The Bible tells us what is important to God, so those things ought to be our guidelines for His will.

died in his early fifties of heart problems after spending twenty years witnessing to the Pokots. He died feeling like a failure because there was almost no response to all of his preaching.

But the hope of this missionary was so evident in his life that his children followed in his footsteps. In fact, his son, Malcom, was so impressed with his father's heart for the people of Kenya, that he joined Africa Inland Mission to be a missionary in Kenya.

There have been quite a few technological advancements since Tom Collins died. A present missionary to the Pokots, Art Davis, doesn't have to search for the nomadic tribe by foot. Instead he flies across North Kenya by helicopter. On one afternoon

The same message about this Jesus of the Bible.

last year, he spotted several Pokot herdsmen and landed his heli-copter nearby. He set up a mobile clinic under the shade of a large thorn tree nearby.

By the late afternoon, a fairly large group had assembled to receive medical treatment at Davis' temporary clinic and to hear what the missionary had to say. The gospel message was presented, but there was no response from the crowd. Then a withered old man, obviously one of the elder statesmen of the group, rose to his feet and said: "Fifty years ago a missionary named Tom Collins told us the same message about this Jesus of the Bible. And it was under this very same tree where he talked to us. We refused to believe what he said back then because our witchdoctors and elders forbade it. Since that time, we have suffered greatly. Our herds have died. Our children have starved. Our gods have let us down. As for me and my wives and children, today we will follow this Jesus you are telling us about. In Him there is hope. "

Art Davis did not realize until that very moment that he was standing under the very thorn tree where Tom Collins had stood fifty years before. The scenery was the same. The message of hope was the same. But the hearts of the Pokots had changed. They were ready to receive the message of God's love.

There were "ooh's" and "aah's" heard around the table as Jim finished his story. We noticed a few tears well up in several eyes (ours included). There is nothing more amazing than a story of hope that perseveres in the face of adversity. Jim probably knew that. He also knew enough to tell his story last.

The Statue of Liberty in New York City.

Bruce strikes up a conversation with a tourist.

OUR TRIP ACROSS AMERICA · BRUCE & STAN

MILWAUKEE
Racine
Kenosha
Waukegan
Evanston
CHICAGO

Sheboygan

Muskegon
Kalamazoo

Fort Wayne

Kokomo

Hope Springs Eternal

It may seem a little strange to associate hope with a baseball team, but if you're a Chicago Cubs fan, it's the most natural thing in the world.

The Chicago Cubs are one of Major League Baseball's oldest teams, and they're also one of the losingest. Since they were founded in 1876, the Cubs have played more than 18,000 games. Yet the last time they won a World Series—the ultimate sign of success in baseball—was in 1908. Their most recent National League pennant came more than half a century ago in 1945, the same year World War II ended. But don't feel sorry for this team of sad sacks. Despite the longest championship drought in professional sports history, the Cubs have an amazing fan following. The people of Chicago may not live and die by what the Cubs do on the field, but make no mistake about it—they love their Cubbies.

We didn't get the opportunity to see the Chicago Cubs play when we were in Chicago, but playoff fever was in the air. It was only July, mind you (the post season doesn't start until September), but the Cubs were in the middle of an amazing winning streak. They had been playing well of late and were coming very close to breaking .500, that magic percentage in which wins equal losses. It had been a long time since the Cubs were this close to having a winning record this late in the season. Their improbable success was having such an effect on the locals, that otherwise normal people were absolutely giddy with "what ifs."

What if the Cubs keep this streak going? What if they don't fall apart like they always do in the second half of the season? What if they get into the playoffs? What if I win the lottery?

The great thing about "What if" questions is that they show an indomitable spirit and a special perseverance that can only be summarized in the word *hope*. Sometimes you put your hope in things or events you know are going to happen. This kind of hope is rooted in reality. Then there's the Chicago Cubs kind of hope. This kind of hope is more like a wish; reality has very little to do with it. But it's still hope, and it's the kind that often gets us through some hard times.

Hope is the power of
being cheerful in circumstances
which we know to
be desperate.

G.K. CHESTERTON

Cub fans know about hard times, yet they never give up hope. Yeah, their loyalty may have something to do with Wrigley Field, the Cubs' home since 1914. Chicago Cubs fans will tell you that there's not a more pleasurable (and affordable) experience than sitting behind the ivy-covered walls in the outfield bleachers on a sunny Chicago afternoon. Now a baseball stadium can't do anything more than sit there and look pretty. But the Cubs, now that's a different story. The Cubs can take you near the point of wish-fulfillment, like they were doing when we visited Chicago. Or they can break your heart, just like they've done for the last century or so.

Still, there's reason for hope. As the season winds down each year, the rallying cry of every Cubs fan is "There's always next year." And when the club gets ready for the new season, the mantra becomes, "Hope springs eternal."

Ah, to be a Cubs fan. Oh, to have such hope!

Hope Held Captive

We visited lots of churches when we were on our cross-country trip. (There isn't much else to do on a Sunday morning when you're in a place like Omaha, Nebraska.) Don't get us wrong; we didn't mind. In fact, we like going to different churches, and we enjoy participating in the various styles of worship. Every church seems to have its own personality when it comes to worshiping God. They all do it a little differently.

When you go to a new church, you expect to see something new. That's part of the fun of it, and looking around at the new surroundings can keep you awake during a slow-paced sermon. Because you are anticipating things to be different, you don't expect to be shocked by anything.

But that's exactly what might happen if you were sitting on the aisle at the Community Bible Church when a particular usher stops at your row to pass the offering plate. The offering plates won't startle you (there is nothing unusual about them), but the tattoos on the forearms of Fred Mendrin might.

In some churches, Fred might not have the opportunity to be an usher. His tattoos aren't offensive (they are tastefully drawn portraits of a woman), but some people might worry that the tattoos could be distracting. (We'll admit that Bruce was caught off-guard when he went to reach for the offering plate and saw the face of a woman on a hairy arm.) We suppose the problem could be solved if Fred just wore long-sleeved shirts all the time. But the folks at Community Bible Church don't find Fred's tattoos to be distracting. Just the opposite. Those tattoos remind them of Fred's story and the kind of man he *used* to be. It's an interesting story, and it's all about the hope that comes from God's power to transform a life.

To the people at Community Bible Church, Fred is a big teddy bear. Actually, a *huge* teddy bear. His laughter and smile are infectious. You would only need to spend a few minutes with him, and you'd be convinced that he was a gentle giant. That's quite a transformation for a man who was once considered one of the most dangerous inmates in the California maximum-security prison system.

The recurring theme during the first three decades of Fred's life was insecurity. He constantly struggled to prove himself and impress others. Although he had natural athletic ability (he earned nine varsity letters in three years in high school in football, basketball, and baseball), that wasn't enough. He wanted to prove to the world that he was mean and tough.

The alcohol use began at age fourteen. That was quickly followed by further substance abuse: barbiturates, marijuana, and other drugs. By the time he dropped out of high school in April of his senior year, Fred was using heroin and LSD. The next few years were filled with more drugs, theft, hot credit cards, and robbery. When people asked what he was doing with his life, Fred would say: "I'm working my way to prison." He was right.

Fred was arrested in 1969 for possession of one-half ounce of marijuana. He was sentenced to prison

Fred, in shackles, as a prison gang member.

for six months to ten years. He actually looked forward to his incarceration so he could earn the reputation of being a hardcore prisoner.

Because of the non-violent nature of his offense, Fred was sent to the Sierra Conservation Center where inmates are taught to fight forest fires. Fred didn't need to learn the fighting part. He was there just a few weeks when he instigated a race riot among the prisoners. Consequently, he was transferred to a higher security prison in Tracy and placed in a segregation unit. This began Fred's tour of the maximum prison facilities in California where he spent the next nine years in isolation from the general inmate population.

While in the Tracy facility, Fred made connections with the leaders of an infamous prison gang. It was Fred's goal to become a part of this gang so others would fear and respect him as one of the toughest convicts. The gang officially accepted him when he was transferred to the segregation unit at Chino. As he heard the stories of past exploits of the meanest members of his new gang, he fantacized about the day new gang members would be listening to stories of his heinous deeds.

By March of 1972, Fred had already served two years on his possession of marijuana charge. He was scheduled to appear before his parole board in six months, with the likelihood of being released before the end of the year. But that wouldn't happen. Fred was given an assignment by his gang to kill another inmate who had offended one of the gang brothers. Knowing that he would jeopardize his chance of ever getting out of prison, Fred balked at the assignment and suggested that he could be of more value to the gang on the outside. The gang spread rumors about his reluctance, and Fred agreed to commit the killing in order to protect his hardcore image.

In an elaborate and well-choreographed plan, Fred

God's grace doesn't operate on
some sort of sliding scale,
whereby some of us get more
grace than others.

trapped his prey in a room and stabbed him to death with a prison-made knife. Fred kept stabbing his victim until the prison guards restrained him. Within nine months, he was found guilty of first-degree murder and sentenced to a prison term of seven years to life. He had been only a few months away from freedom, but now he faced the prospect of never enjoying freedom again.

Following his murder conviction, Fred was transferred to San Quentin State Prison and placed in "the hole." This area was home to California's most defiant, actively violent and nonconforming inmates. Fred had made it to the top. He finally had the reputation he had longed for. He was a cruel, cold-blooded killer. But instead of being proud of this image, he felt nothing but emptiness.

Even though Fred was confined to his cell for twenty-three and one-half hours a day, the gang fights and the drug use continued. Once Fred managed to unlatch the door of his cell and attack an inmate who was walking by. Fred didn't even know the inmate. The inmate survived the attack, even though Fred stabbed him thirty times with a four-inch blade before the guards intervened.

Fred didn't always come out the victor in these prison fights. He lost big time in April 1976 (but this loss proved to be the turning point in his life). Fred had been transported from San Quentin to the Los Angeles County Jail to testify as a witness in the trial of another inmate. In the jail, two members of an enemy gang overpowered him and he suffered multiple wounds as they stabbed him with his own weapon.

Fred could see Catalina Island from his bed in the jail hospital. That's when a switch flipped inside him. He realized what he was missing in the outside world. He also realized that his tough-man reputation could get him killed, and he would be the talk of the prison for only a few days before he was forgotten. In a moment of desperation, Fred cried out to God: "Lord have mercy on me. I believe you. Change my life. I'm tired of the same old madness." As he spoke these words, Fred felt a sudden sense of peace and calmness.

Fred's transformation was immediate. He felt the difference, and those around him noticed a difference. One officer described it this way: "I don't want to say it was a miracle, but I guess it was. Never in my twenty-five years with law enforcement have I seen anybody who has made such a dramatic change."

Fred was transferred back to the prison in Chino where he started reading the Bible. He also spoke with the prison chaplain whenever possible and was allowed to attend prison Bible study groups. The Chino prison was where Fred had joined his gang. Now he was back in Chino where he disavowed his gang membership, and began counseling younger inmates against joining gangs.

Within two years after his transformation, he was reassigned to the prison in Chino (still kept in maximum-security housing). Although there was absolutely no basis for it, Fred had hope for the immediate future. That means he had hope he could survive in prison without being killed. The odds were against it. He had attacked or made enemies of the most notorious leaders of opposing gangs. And he had turned his back on his own gang—the ultimate offense

within the brotherhood. Fred was a vulnerable target for retaliation by both his former foes and his former friends.

Even more amazing, Fred had hope for his long-range future. That means he had hope for an eventual release from prison although he was serving a potential life-sentence for murder and had a horrendous record of behavior following that conviction. It was not the kind of record that inclined a parole board toward early release. Nonetheless, he had hope.

Fred displayed this overwhelming sense of hope for his future when he asked permission of prison authorities to speak with other inmates who might be harboring hatred against him. Fred wanted to ask their forgiveness. He was given permission and his efforts brought a sense of peace and reconciliation to that violent atmosphere.

From Chino, Fred was transferred to a correctional facility in Vacaville considered to have little gang influence. Nonetheless, to ensure his protection, Fred remained isolated from the general population until 1980. Then, in 1984, after an exemplary record of behavior in the general inmate population, the parole board gave Fred a 1988 parole date (with the possibility of an earlier release). The assignment of a parole date wasn't the only good thing that happened to Fred in 1984.

That same year he became the head clerk for the prison chaplain who had been watching Fred mature as a Christian. He also continued leading a Bible study and counseling

Fred, the family man, with Susanna and their daughters.

other inmates. With this background, Fred was selected to meet with several seminary students whose course work included training in a prison setting. One of these students was Sue Stierer. As Fred and Sue got to know each other better during the weekly sessions, it became clear to both of them that they were feeling an emotional, physical and spiritual attraction to each other.

Let's fast forward through Fred's story to the day of his release. After an incarceration of nearly twenty-two years, Fred walked out of prison. But his exit from the correctional facility had much more panache than other prisoners who are released. Fred was wearing a tuxedo. And that same afternoon, he was married to Sue.

———————

Fifteen years have passed since Fred was released from prison. The hope that he sensed in that jail hospital bed looking out on Catalina Island has been realized. Today, Fred and Susanna Mendrin—and their two daughters— live a life that has no appearance or connection with Fred's past as one of the most feared inmates at San Quentin. In fact, if you met friendly Fred at the Community Bible

Church, or if he passed you an offering plate, you wouldn't even have a clue about his sordid past . . . except for those tattoos that were emblazoned on his forearms by a fellow inmate. And if you asked about those tattoos, Fred or anyone from the Community Bible Church family would be glad to tell you what they represent: a story of hope in a God who can transform a life.

Hoping Against the Odds

We concluded our cross-country trip in Las Vegas. There is no correlation between Vegas being the gambling capital of the world and being the final destination on our journey. Sure, our money ran out there, but that was according to a precisely calculated budget. It had nothing to do with gambling, because each of us hates to lose money at a rate faster than we can make it.

But the other tourists in Vegas did not share our lack of enthusiasm for gambling. They were passionate about it. You might even say that some of them were desperate about it.

Even though we didn't gamble, we enjoyed hanging out at the roulette tables for two reasons:

When you meet
someone with no hope,
remember that only Jesus
can give the hope that
person needs.

- First, we discovered that if you stand close to the real gamblers, the waitresses will think you're a "player" and bring you free soft drinks. (This is particularly convenient when you've reached the end of your precisely calculated budget.)

- Secondly, we enjoyed watching the distressed gamblers as they sank deeper into despair. (We're sadistic like that.)

So, our entertainment for one evening included chugging down complimentary diet soft drinks while we watched the color drain out of the faces of people standing around the roulette table. The later the evening got, the more pale they became. We called it quits when it looked like we were standing with a group of albinos.

It was that experience that taught us an important lesson about hope. All of those people were *hoping* to hit it big. But *hoping* is different than *hope:*

- Their hoping was a matter of playing against the odds.

On that particular evening, most of the hoping proved to be hopeless.

- Hope, on the other hand, doesn't concern itself with the odds. True hope is based on the confident reliance of something, or someone, who has proven to be faithful in the past. Based on such past experience, there can be hope for the future.

Our albino friends could have learned a valuable lesson from us non-gamblers that night. The only thing that proved to be trustworthy and reliable was the waitress who kept bringing us sodas. (Maybe the casino manager thought we were "bad luck" and wanted us to keep standing by his roulette table.)

Stan offers thanks to the Pilgrims for sailing to America in 1620.

OUR TRIP ACROSS AMERICA
BRUCE & STAN

We first met Hope Lauren Guthrie at a convention in Nashville. It was a gathering of Christian publishers, retailers, and people who have the audacity to write down words for a book so other people can be inspired. We say *audacity* only when it applies to people like us, because we've never considered ourselves great writers, or really writers at all. Great writers are like artists who skillfully assemble words and phrases into sentences that move others deeply. Writing books is a humbling process for us, because it demonstrates (to us at least) how inadequate we really are. Our words are sometimes rather clumsy, and our jokes usually fall flat, but that's not what this is all about. Our words are merely the means to talk about the extraordinary people we meet and the stories they tell.

We're simply two guys who enjoy observing cultural trends and human nature, and we try to see how it all fits into the framework of a Christian worldview. That's why these stories are so important to us. More than introducing you to some interesting characters we've met along the way, we hope they move you in some manner that says, "I want to do better," or "Perhaps God can use me in the same way He used that person."

The story of Hope is one of the most powerful we have ever heard. We feel inadequate to even tell it to you, but this book would not be complete without it.

We actually didn't expect to meet Hope. We had an appointment with Hope's mother, Nancy, a publicist and writer who works in Christian publishing and lives in Nashville with her husband, David and her son, Matt.

Hope is hearing the melody of the future.
Faith is to dance to it.

RUBEM ALVES

During the convention Nancy was working out of one of those temporary offices, the kind they set up in a meeting room for the people who oversee the details of conventions and conferences. There were desks and phones and partitions set up, and Nancy was working her corner of the room like the professional that she is.

After some small talk, we asked Nancy how she was doing, and then we asked about Hope, born a little more than two months earlier with a rare metabolic disorder called Zellweger syndrome. We had heard about Hope's condition, and the fact that children afflicted with this malady usually live less than six months. Nancy said she was doing well, and that she very much appreciated the prayers of so many people. Then she said something that rather surprised us. "Do you want to meet Hope?"

You would think that a child born with a fatal disorder would be in the hospital with tubes running every which way and doctors scurrying about with clipboards and such. At least that's what we imagined. Hope had been through a regimen like that (only with much more technical medical procedures than we have described), but now she was with her mother and family full-time, and that's the way it would remain. "Follow me," Nancy said warmly. "Hope is behind that partition."

We followed Nancy and came upon the most beautiful sight we had ever seen. There, lying sweetly in her grandmother's arms was Hope, so tiny, so frail, so very helpless, yet with the most amazing expression on her face. Our words cannot possibly do that moment justice, and we

If you do not hope,
you will not find out
what is beyond
your hopes.

CLEMENT OF ALEXANDRIA

"For I know the plans I have for you," says the Lord. *"They are plans for good and not for disaster, to give you a future and a hope."*

JEREMIAH 29:11

---

cannot begin to adequately describe the way Hope looked. The best we can say is that it was heavenly.

It was the face that touched us, like a living symbol of her name. Normally the face of a two-month old baby reflects little more than natural physical feelings, and these generally revolve around food, comfort, and sleep. Hope had a much different expression on her tender face. Clearly it was one of expectancy, like you might have if you know something very special is going to happen to you. Her little lips were pursed together sweetly, and the corners of her mouth edged up ever so slightly. Her delicate eyes gazed at her grandmother, who held her tenderly, patting her frail body. You couldn't look at Hope without pausing to reflect: what thoughts and emotions had settled in her infant mind to produce such a countenance?

In those few moments we had with Hope, we realized that she was not merely a child; she was a teacher. She didn't utter a sound, and yet her life spoke volumes to us about the nature of hope itself. Inherent in the definition of hope is the feeling that something desirable is about to happen. The Scriptures tell of hope in the context of faith, which is the "confident assurance that what we hope for is going to happen" (Heb. 11:1). Was it possible that little Hope, who was born with a physical shell that would soon give her up to eternity, had the assurance that she would soon be in a far, far better place? We had no doubt that she did.

Over the next few months Hope would touch literally thousands of people. Nancy and David are busy people, and they are family people. They were determined to take Hope with them to every activity and gathering, knowing that each moment was precious. Hope had a lot of birthday celebrations because Nancy and David knew her life would be measured in months, not years. She also accompanied her parents to meet-ings, hymn sings, Bibles studies, and

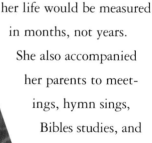

She was a gift to all of us.

Death is not the end of your life's story:
it is just the end of a chapter.

fellowship groups. No doubt Hope took it all in, comforted and held by many tender arms, but can you imagine the gift she gave to everyone who saw her as we did? Can you picture the impact of this little one sharing her gift of hope with others?

Hope's time on earth lasted a mere 199 days. For most of us that period of time goes by in a blur. But for Hope and her family, it was a lifetime lived to its absolute fullest. At her memorial service the pastor said this of Hope's life on earth: "Because God is who He is, Hope's life accomplished far more than we could ever comprehend, far more than a host of people who have lived three score and ten. Hope was a gift from God. We didn't realize how precious a gift she was. And she was not only a gift to David and Nancy and Matthew and her grandparents; she was a gift to all of us. It was amazing how God worked through that little girl."

We merely stood on the fringes of Hope's life for a few minutes, but we were one of those who received her gift. Our hope is that in some small way, we have been able to pass on that gift to you.

AMAZING GRACE

When we've been there

ten thousand years

Bright shining as the sun,

We've no less days to sing God's praise

Than when we've first begun!

OUR TRIP ACROSS AMERICA

BRUCE & STAN

The Hope of Heaven

Not long after Hope Guthrie went to be with the Lord, we received a tape of her memorial service. Nancy graciously sent it to us so we could share in Hope's life completely. You see, when you measure time against eternity, the short time Hope spent on earth was no different than the years the rest of us are allotted. Hope lived for six months, and someone else may live six decades. The amount of time we live on this temporary home called earth matters little, because life "is like the morning fog—it's here a little while, then it's gone" (James 4:14). What matters is the time we live in our permanent home called heaven.

Like you, we believe in heaven. We believe it's a real place. But we must admit that we don't think about heaven

People nowadays take time more seriously than eternity.

THOMAS KELLY

---

all that much. There are so many cares and concerns and opportunities in this world, and heaven seems so far away. How foolish we are! Don't we realize that in a matter of moments—if you measure our time against eternity— everything we call important is going to fade away, and that which we've set aside is going to become our over- whelming reality?

Sometimes it takes the words of a compelling speaker or a great book to wake us up to the reality of heaven. Little did we realize when we began listening to the tape of Hope's ongoing story that we would have both to remind us of the greatest hope of all—the hope of heaven.

The compelling speaker was Anne Graham Lotz (yes, *that* Anne Graham Lotz, the daughter of Billy Graham), and the great book was the Bible. The fact that Anne was present at Hope's memorial service was another surprise in a story of great surprises. Even more, it was a stirring testimony to the impact this precious little one had on people everywhere. The fact that Anne opened the Scriptures to tell God's story of hope was no surprise; the Grahams have always relied on God's Word to proclaim the Good News that Jesus is the only way for us to find the hope of heaven.

"If you have placed your faith in Jesus Christ as your Savior and Lord, if you're a child of God," Anne began, "then you're just a stranger in this world. You're just a pilgrim passing through. Heaven is your real home. Heaven has been prepared as a love gift for those who have a personal relationship with Jesus. Hope's home is one that has been prepared for her—and for us—in love and in great detail by Jesus."

Anne Graham Lotz opened our eyes to this wonderful place. As we listened to the tape, our vision of heaven as God's love gift began to grow. Anne described the Taj Mahal, that great wonder of the world built in Agra, India by the emperor Shah Jahan in the seventeenth century as a memorial to his wife. It took 22,000 workers more than twenty years to construct this magnificent building. What an incredible labor of love. Yet as Anne reminded us, "how much more is the place Jesus is preparing for us, His bride—and He's been at it 2,000 years" (John 14:2).

When Hope entered heaven, she knew instantly that she was expected, and she was welcome. "She knew heaven had been prepared just for her, because Jesus had prepared the things that she would enjoy and that would make her feel that she belonged there," Anne said. Not only has

I pray that your hearts
will be flooded with light so
that you can understand the
wonderful future he has
promised to those he called.
I want you to realize what a
rich and glorious inheritance he
has given to his people.

EPHESIANS 1:18

heaven been prepared for Hope, it has also been prepared for our hope, and it has been prepared perfectly.

On the tape Anne talked about heaven as a perfect place where there will be no more *separation.* The instant we are ushered into heaven, we will no longer experience disappointment, hurt feelings, misunderstandings, divorce, or death. There will be no more wars, refugee camps, ethnic cleansing, racial prejudice, or different religions. At long last, we're going to be together with God.

In heaven there will be no scars that come with life and living. Everything will be new. "The only scars in heaven will be the scars on the hands and the feet and in the side of Jesus to remind us always of the grace of God and what it cost Him to offer heaven to us as our home."

In heaven there will be no more *suffering.* "No blindness, no deafness, no lameness, no sickness, no diabetes, no arthritis, no Parkinson's, no cataracts, no strokes, no cancer, and no Zellweger syndrome," Anne continued. "There will be no pain and no hospitals and no funerals and no grave. Heaven will hold no tears. There will be no broken hearts and no broken hopes of what might have been, because heaven is the place of ultimate hope."

We sat speechless as we finished the tape, realizing that it's one thing to believe in heaven, and quite another to believe it's your greatest hope. We realized how attached we have become to this present world and how little we think about heaven.

On the other hand, we understood that some of the longings that often fill the human heart can never be satisfied by the things of earth. C. S. Lewis wrote: "If I find in myself a desire which no experience in this world can satisfy, the most probably explanation is that I was made for another world."

Finally, we were amazed that it took the brief life of a

little baby named Hope to remind us of the incredible place of hope Jesus has prepared just for us.

> "No eye has seen, nor ear has heard,
> and no mind has imagined
> what God has prepared
> for those who love him."
> —1 Corinthians 2:9

This is the real
significance of death: Not that
it is the finale to life, but that it is
the end of your opportunity to
make a choice for God.

GOD IS IN THE SMALL STUFF
FOR YOUR FAMILY

More Stories

We invite you to read some of the other stories
we heard in the course of our cross-country tour of America.
They have been collected in three additional books:

Stories We Heard About Love
Stories We Heard About Joy
Stories We Heard About Courage

And here are some other books we've written,
some of which are quoted in this one:

God Is in the Small Stuff
God Is in the Small Stuff For Your Family
onyourown.com
Bruce & Stan's Guide to God
Bruce & Stan Search for the Meaning of Life

We'd love to hear from you. You can reach us by email at
guide@bruceandstan.com or through our Web site:
www.bruceandstan.com.